15.95

Grasshoppers

Grasshoppers

Mary Ann McDonald

THE CHILD'S WORLD®, INC.

Library of Congress Cataloging-in-Publication Data
McDonald, Mary Ann.
Grasshoppers / by Mary Ann McDonald.
p.   cm.
Includes index.
Summary: Briefly describes the physical characteristics,
behavior, and life cycle of different kinds of grasshoppers.
ISBN 1-56766-505-5 (lib. bdg. : alk paper)
1. Grasshoppers—Juvenile literature.
[1. Grasshoppers.]   I. Title.
QL508.A2M185   1998
595.7'26—dc21   97-44644
CIP
AC

Photo Credits

ANIMALS ANIMALS © D.R. Specker: 19
ANIMALS ANIMALS © K. G. Preston-Mafham: 20
© Charles Krebs/Tony Stone Images: 24
© Joe McDonald: 6
© John R. Patton: 16
© Kevin Schafer: cover
© Robert and Linda Mitchell: 2, 10, 15, 23, 26, 29, 30
© 1996 Skip Moody/Dembinsky Photo Assoc. Inc: 9
© 1997 Skip Moody/Dembinsky Photo Assoc. Inc: 13

On the cover...

Front cover: This colorful grasshopper lives in Africa.
Page 2: *Forest grasshoppers* like this one are very beautiful.

Table of Contents

On a sunny summer day, you go walking in a grassy field. The tall grass waves in the breeze, and birds call in the distance. Suddenly, you see a small insect jump in the grass near you. You look closely. What could it be? It's a grasshopper!

⇐ This *lubber grasshopper* is resting on a leafy branch.

What Are Grasshoppers?

Grasshoppers are a kind of **insect**. Insects have bodies with three parts—a head, a chest (called the **thorax**), and a belly (called the **abdomen**). They also have six legs. Grasshoppers belong to the same insect family as crickets, locusts, and katydids. They all live in warm areas such as deserts, grasslands, meadows, and woodlands.

Most grasshoppers fly well. They have a pair of sturdy wings near the front of their bodies, and another pair of large, clear wings near the back. Grasshoppers are also good jumpers. Their back legs are long and specially made for leaping. The ends of the legs have little hooks to provide a strong grip.

Southeastern lubber grasshoppers like this one are very colorful. ⇒

Are There Different Kinds of Grasshoppers?

There are many different kinds of grasshoppers. Most of them fall within two groups—*short-horned grasshoppers* and *long-horned grasshoppers*. All of them have feelers, called **antennae**, on their heads. The grasshopper touches things with its antennae to learn about its surroundings. Short-horned grasshoppers get their name from their short antennae. Long-horned grasshoppers have antennae that are very long.

⇐ *Rainbow grasshoppers* like this one are short-horned grasshoppers.

How Do Grasshoppers Make Noise?

Grasshoppers are some of the best singers in the insect world. They "sing" by scraping one body part against another. One of the body parts, called the *scraper*, has a sharp edge. The other, called the *file*, has hard ridges. Rubbing the scraper across the file makes a loud sound. Different kinds of grasshoppers make different sounds. They also have different "songs" for calling females, challenging other males, and sounding an alarm.

It is easy to see the files on the back of this grasshopper's leg. ⇒

Short-horned grasshoppers have their files on their back legs. Their scrapers are on the edges of their front wings. To make chirping sounds, they rub a leg over a wing. The *band-winged grasshopper* even makes a sound when it flies! It snaps its wings and makes a crackling sound as it flies through the air.

Long-horned grasshoppers have files and scrapers on their front wings. They make noise by raising their wings into the air and rubbing them back and forth.

This *band-wing grasshopper* is resting on some rocks in Arizona. ⇒

How Are Baby Grasshoppers Born?

The male grasshopper "sings" to attract a female. After they mate, the female lays eggs through a special egg-laying tube called an **ovipositor**. Long-horned grasshoppers have a long, curved ovipositor that they use to slit open plants. Then they lay a row of eggs inside the plant. Short-horned grasshoppers have a short ovipositor. They use it to dig a hole in the ground. Then they lay their eggs in clumps at the bottom of the hole.

⇐ This female *differential grasshopper* is laying her eggs in the ground.

When the eggs hatch, baby insects crawl out. These babies, called **nymphs**, look like adults, only much smaller. But unlike adults, the nymphs cannot fly. It takes several months for each nymph to grow into an adult. During that time, the nymph eats plants to grow bigger and stronger.

This young grasshopper nymph is resting on a leaf. ⇒

Grasshopper nymphs do not have skin that grows, as yours does. Instead, the nymph must **molt**, or shed its outer layer of skin, as it gets bigger. When the old skin gets too small, it splits down the back, and the nymph pushes its way out. A newer, bigger skin is waiting underneath.

What Do Grasshoppers Eat?

Short-horned grasshoppers eat only plants. Sometimes they eat every plant, grass, or vegetable in sight! Long-horned grasshoppers eat plants too, but they also eat other insects. The mouth parts of grasshoppers are made for biting and chewing. Sometimes even clothing and screen doors are not safe from hungry grasshoppers.

This *bird grasshopper* is eating a piece of grass. ⇒

Grasshoppers and their relatives have damaged more crops and other plants than any other animal in history. Sometimes billions of grasshoppers get together in huge groups. Then they jump and fly over hundreds of miles of land, eating all the plants in their path.

⇐ These southeastern lubber grasshoppers are gathering in a field.

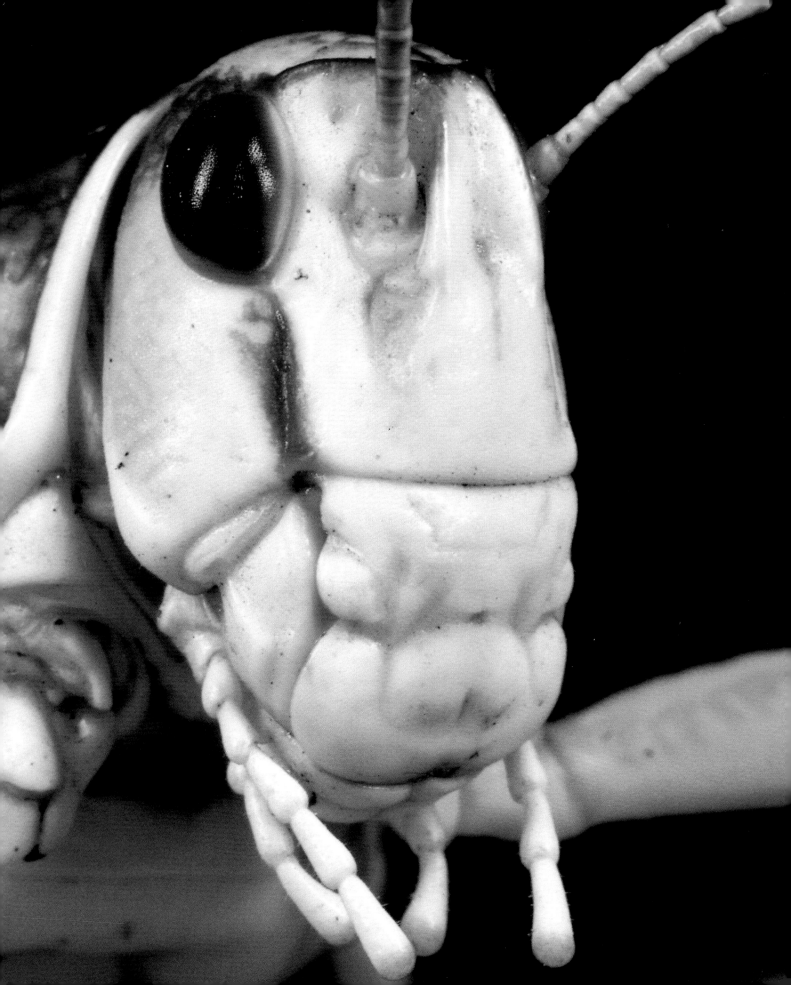

How Do Grasshoppers Stay Safe?

Grasshoppers have many enemies. Birds and other animals love to make tasty meals of grasshoppers. Some grasshoppers depend on their coloring to hide them from enemies. Others jump or fly away, showing their brightly colored wings as they flee. This sudden burst of color confuses the enemy and gives the grasshoppers extra time to get away. One grasshopper, called the *lubber grasshopper*, uses a different kind of protection. When it is frightened, it oozes a stinky foam from its mouth and body! This foam helps keep other animals at a distance.

⇐ This *western lubber grasshopper* protects itself with foam.

How Can You Study Grasshoppers?

During the summertime, it's easy to study grasshoppers. You can walk into a meadow or field and sweep the grass with a large butterfly net. You might even catch several different kinds. If you have an insect book, you might be able to find out what kind they are before you let them go.

This differential grasshopper is bright yellow. ⇒

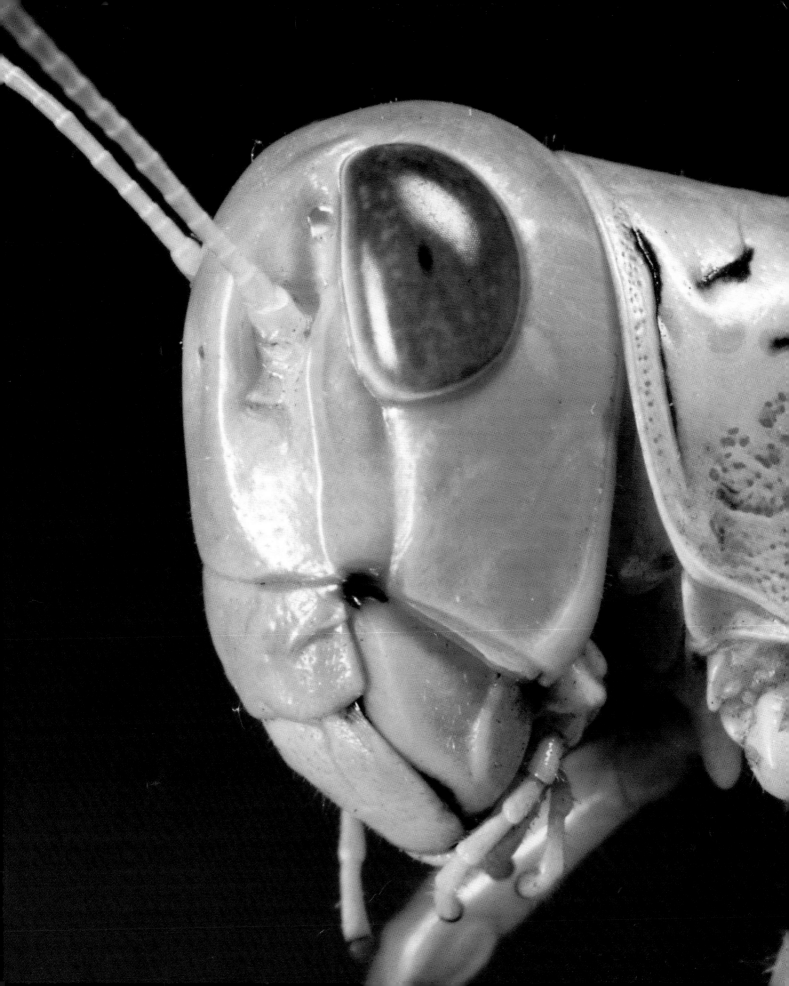

We often think of grasshoppers and their relatives as pests, but they really are fascinating creatures. They are also a natural part of the world around us. So the next time you are hiking through a sunny meadow, stop for a moment and listen for the grasshoppers. Can you recognize their songs?

Glossary

abdomen (AB–doh–men)
The abdomen is the belly area of an insect. Grasshoppers have a skinny abdomen.

antennae (an–TEH–nee)
Antennae are the feelers on an insect's head. Grasshoppers use their antennae to touch and learn about the world around them.

insect (IN–sekt)
Insects are animals that have six legs and a body divided into three parts. Grasshoppers are insects.

molt (MOLT)
Molting is shedding an old, outgrown skin. Grasshopper nymphs molt several times before they become adults.

nymph (NIMF)
A nymph is a baby insect. A grasshopper nymph looks like a little adult grasshopper.

ovipositor (oh–vih–PAH–zih–ter)
An ovipositor is a special egg-laying tube that some insects have. Katydids have long, curved ovipositors that slit open plants to lay eggs inside.

thorax (THOR–ax)
The chest area of an insect is called the thorax.

Index